Instant Java Password and Authentication Security

A practical, hands-on guide to securing Java application passwords with hashing techniques

Fernando Mayoral

BIRMINGHAM - MUMBAI

Instant Java Password and Authentication Security

First published: November 2013

Production Reference: 1221113

Published by Packt Publishing Ltd.
Livery Place
35 Livery Street
Birmingham B3 2PB, UK.

ISBN 978-1-84969-776-7

www.packtpub.com

Credits

Author
Fernando Mayoral

Reviewers
Benjamin Bahrenburg
Rahul Bhattacharjee

Acquisition Editor
Edward Gordan
Taron Pereira

Commissioning Editor
Neil Alexander

Technical Editor
Nadeem N. Bagban

Copy Editors
Roshni Banerjee
Dipti Kapadia

Project Coordinator
Ankita Goenka

Proofreader
Lucy Rowland

Production Coordinator
Kyle Albuquerque

Cover Work
Kyle Albuquerque

Cover Image
Sheetal Aute

About the Author

Fernando Mayoral is a young app developer and an advanced student in Systems Engineering, with experience in distributed systems, data mining, high performance algorithms, and web security. He is a web security enthusiast, always trying to learn as much as possible.

Fernando has taken part in very interesting startups, personal projects, and full time jobs. He has worked on big projects for Cardif, a multinational insurance company that is part of the BNP Paribas group, and has collaborated indirectly on projects for Toyota and Pan American Energy.

I would like to thank the entire Packt Publishing team for this opportunity and for their support and patience. It's amazing to be able to pass on some things I've learned over the years.

About the Reviewers

Benjamin Bahrenburg is an author, blogger, and technology director. Ben specializes in building enterprise solutions using Mobile Technologies, Geo Location Services, and Domain Specific Languages. Over the last decade, he has provided enterprise mobility solutions for numerous Fortune 100 organizations. Ben is a published writer, having authored several articles and the Packt book, *Appcelerator Titanium Business Application Development Cookbook*, which provides the best practices and recipes for successful Enterprise cross-platform mobile development.

Ben spends much of his time blogging and speaking about mobile, enterprise, and open source development at `http://bencoding.com`. You can also reach him on Twitter at `http://twitter.com/bencoding`.

Rahul Bhattacharjee has more than nine years of experience in designing and architecting software systems. He is currently working as an engineer with Yahoo! India engineering team (Ad platforms). He is a BE degree holder from the National Institute of Technology, Durgapur and holds numerous technical certifications.

www.PacktPub.com

Support files, eBooks, discount offers and more

You might want to visit www.PacktPub.com for support files and downloads related to your book.

Did you know that Packt offers eBook versions of every book published, with PDF and ePub files available? You can upgrade to the eBook version at www.PacktPub.com and as a print book customer, you are entitled to a discount on the eBook copy. Get in touch with us at service@packtpub.com for more details.

At www.PacktPub.com, you can also read a collection of free technical articles, sign up for a range of free newsletters and receive exclusive discounts and offers on Packt books and eBooks.

http://PacktLib.PacktPub.com

Do you need instant solutions to your IT questions? PacktLib is Packt's online digital book library. Here, you can access, read and search across Packt's entire library of books.

Why Subscribe?

- Fully searchable across every book published by Packt
- Copy and paste, print and bookmark content
- On demand and accessible via web browser

Free Access for Packt account holders

If you have an account with Packt at www.PacktPub.com, you can use this to access PacktLib today and view nine entirely free books. Simply use your login credentials for immediate access.

Table of Contents

Preface

In this book you will learn how to create strong and secure hashes to protect sensitive passwords and keys.

With the evolution of technology and communications, there is a lot of information flowing everywhere. Since passwords keep our sensitive data secure, password security has become a critical issue, now more than ever, especially with so many malicious hackers trying to take advantage.

There is no such thing as a fully secure web application, there's always a flaw somewhere waiting to be patched—or exploited. However, there is a well-tested technique that allows us to create a last barrier against intrusions: hashing. By hashing our passwords properly, we can protect our users from hackers. This makes it very hard (almost impossible) for hackers to gain access to their accounts. This technique and some useful hints will be covered in this book.

What this book covers

Creating a simple hash teaches you how to create a basic hash code and how it works.

Creating a strong hash shows you how to create strong hashes using cryptographic secure hash algorithms.

Adding salt to a hash shows the proper use of a salt in order to strengthen the password protection.

Creating a secure hash will teach you how to create the strongest possible hash to provide maximum security to passwords.

The *Overview* section gives a high level overview to round up the whole authentication process.

What you need for this book

The following are the software needed for this book:

- Java Development Kit 1.5 or greater
- Your preferred integrated development environment (Eclipse, NetBeans, and so on)

Who this book is for

This book is targeted for a wide range of people, from people with basic Java knowledge to Java experts. It's assumed that you have some experience in Java and you are interested in learning how to protect your user's information. Even experienced developers must be educated in security in order to write secure applications.

Conventions

In this book, you will find a number of styles of text that distinguish between different kinds of information. Here are some examples of these styles, and an explanation of their meaning.

Code words in text are shown as follows: " Put the password in the MessageDigest."

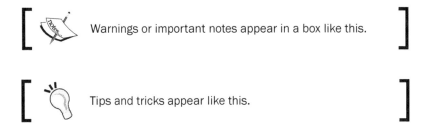

Warnings or important notes appear in a box like this.

Tips and tricks appear like this.

Reader feedback

Feedback from our readers is always welcome. Let us know what you think about this book—what you liked or may have disliked. Reader feedback is important for us to develop titles that you really get the most out of.

To send us general feedback, simply send an e-mail to feedback@packtpub.com, and mention the book title via the subject of your message.

If there is a topic that you have expertise in and you are interested in either writing or contributing to a book, see our author guide on www.packtpub.com/authors.

Customer support

Now that you are the proud owner of a Packt book, we have a number of things to help you to get the most from your purchase.

Downloading the example code

You can download the example code files for all Packt books you have purchased from your account at `http://www.packtpub.com`. If you purchased this book elsewhere, you can visit `http://www.packtpub.com/support` and register to have the files e-mailed directly to you.

Errata

Although we have taken every care to ensure the accuracy of our content, mistakes do happen. If you find a mistake in one of our books—maybe a mistake in the text or the code—we would be grateful if you would report this to us. By doing so, you can save other readers from frustration and help us improve subsequent versions of this book. If you find any errata, please report them by visiting `http://www.packtpub.com/submit-errata`, selecting your book, clicking on the **errata submission form** link, and entering the details of your errata. Once your errata are verified, your submission will be accepted and the errata will be uploaded on our website, or added to any list of existing errata, under the Errata section of that title. Any existing errata can be viewed by selecting your title from `http://www.packtpub.com/support`.

Piracy

Piracy of copyright material on the Internet is an ongoing problem across all media. At Packt, we take the protection of our copyright and licenses very seriously. If you come across any illegal copies of our works, in any form, on the Internet, please provide us with the location address or website name immediately so that we can pursue a remedy.

Please contact us at `copyright@packtpub.com` with a link to the suspected pirated material.

We appreciate your help in protecting our authors, and our ability to bring you valuable content.

Questions

You can contact us at `questions@packtpub.com` if you are having a problem with any aspect of the book, and we will do our best to address it.

Instant Java Password and Authentication Security

Welcome to *Instant Java Password and Authentication Security*. In this book you will learn how to create strong and secure hashes to protect sensitive passwords and keys.

As an introduction, we will learn the basics of hashing using MD5 hashes to get familiarized with the concept.

Later, we will check out the Secure Hash Algorithm, which is a family of standard cryptographic hash functions. After learning the basics, we will see how to protect our hashes against certain types of attacks by salting them—a useful technique.

Of course, malicious hackers are always developing new techniques and technology evolves every day, and to keep up with this, we will learn how to use a very secure technique that allows us to strengthen our hashes over time.

Creating a simple hash (Simple)

This task involves a basic hashing technique to create basic MD5 hashes.

How to do it...

The following are the steps to create the initial hash (Signup):

1. Get the password value as plain text.
2. Get a MD5 `MessageDigest` instance.
3. Put the password in the `MessageDigest` instance.
4. Execute the `digest` method to get the hash byte array.
5. Encode each byte to a Hexadecimal format into a String Builder.
6. Get the built string from the `StringBuilder` function.
7. The built String is a Hexadecimal representation of the MD5 Hash.
8. The password can now be stored.

The following is a screenshot of the code that allows us to perform the steps enumerated before; I've added comments to explain which step we are fulfilling in each piece of code:

```
//1_ Suppose this is the password variable.
String password = "www.packtpub.com";
try {
    //2_ Get a MD5 MessageDigest Instance
    MessageDigest md = MessageDigest.getInstance("MD5");
    //3_ Then add the value's bytes to the MessageDigest
    md.update(password.getBytes());
    //4_ After execute the 'digest' method to get the hash's bytes
    byte byteData[] = md.digest();
    //The byteData array contains the hash bytes in decimal format.
    //in order to represent that hash as a String, we need to encode
    //this byteData array into Hexadecimal format
    //We need a StringBuilder to convert every single byte to a
    //Hexadecimal encoded String
    StringBuilder sb = new StringBuilder();
    // Now, for each byte
    for (int i = 0; i < byteData.length; i++) {
        //5_ Encode the byte to hexadecimal format and append to the String builder
        sb.append(Integer.toString((byteData[i] & 0xff) + 0x100, 16).substring(1));
    }
    //6_ Finally to get the hashed password, get the String Builder
    //buffered values as a String
    return sb.toString();
    //7_ The hashedPassword variable now contains the password's hash as a String
} catch (NoSuchAlgorithmException ex) {
    //This exception is not likely to happen if the "MD5" algorithm's name
    //is correctly spelled in the ".getInstance" method.
    Logger.getLogger("MD5").log(Level.SEVERE, null, ex);
    return null;
}
```

The hashed password can now be saved in the database instead of the plain text password. When the user logs in with his password, we need to create the hash again and compare it with the hash in the database. By doing this, the plain text password is never stored, so nobody knows the original password but the account owner.

How it works...

MD5 is a cryptographic hash function that produces a 128-bit hash value (32 characters in length). It's very simple and straightforward; the basic idea is to map data sets of variable length to data sets of a fixed length. In order to do this, the input message is split into chunks of 512-bit blocks; padding is added so that its length can be divided by 512. Now these blocks are processed by the MD5 algorithm that operates in a 128-bit state and the result will be a 128-bit hash value.

But this algorithm has already been implemented; you only have to use it as in the example code.

Note that two very similar messages processed by the MD5 algorithm will result, most likely, in very different hashes.

Let's wrap the previous code into a function, getHashMD5 (comments removed), as shown in the following screenshot:

```
public static String getHashMD5(String password) {
    try {
        MessageDigest md = MessageDigest.getInstance("MD5");
        md.update(password.getBytes());
        byte byteData[] = md.digest();
        StringBuilder sb = new StringBuilder();
        for (int i = 0; i < byteData.length; i++) {
            sb.append(Integer.toString((byteData[i] & 0xff) + 0x100, 16).substring(1));
        }
        return sb.toString();
    } catch (NoSuchAlgorithmException ex) {
        Logger.getLogger("MD5").log(Level.SEVERE, null, ex);
        return null;
    }
}
```

Now, we can test our MD5 function by running the following code as shown in the screenshot:

```
public static void main(String[] args) {
    String password = "www.packtpub.com";
    System.out.println("Original Value: " + password);
    System.out.println("MD5 Hash: " + getHashMD5(password));
}
```

After executing the preceding code, we will get the following output as shown in the screenshot:

```
Original Value: www.packtpub.com
MD5 Hash: 647d0136520b7d08802df7035dccce01
```

Congratulations! You have successfully generated your first MD5 Hash. I know it's exciting doing this for the first time, however, this is just the introduction, and I want to be very clear about this: never, and I mean never, use MD5 hashes for storing passwords; they are really weak and easy to break.

There's more...

Although MD5 is a widely used hashing algorithm, it is far from being secure since MD5 generates fairly weak hashes.

- The advantages of MD5 hashes are as follows:
    - Easy to implement
    - Very fast in execution and cost-effective in resources
- The disadvantages of MD5 hashes are as follows:
    - MD5 hashes are not collision resistant. This means different passwords can eventually result in the same hash
    - Since it's fast in execution, it's susceptible to brute force and dictionary attacks
    - Rainbow tables with words and generated hashes allow very quick searches for a known hash and also get the original word quickly

Even so, MD5 is useful to check Big Data consistency and it's better than plain text, but it's not a good option to keep really sensitive data (such as passwords) safe.

Password recovery

When we store a hashed password, it's virtually impossible to get the original value, or at least that's the idea. This is because a hash has only one way; unlike encryption, which has two ways (encrypt and decrypt), there is no "de-hash".

So, when a user forgets his password, we can't send him the original password to his e-mail account; instead, we can recover the password in the following two ways:

- Generate a new random password and send it to the user via e-mail, cell phone, and so on. It would be ideal if the system forces the user to change the password after resetting it.
- Generate a link with a code, which allows him to reset his password, and send that link to his e-mail. It's a good idea to make that code expire after a given time frame.

Creating a strong hash (Simple)

This task involves a stronger hashing method to create strong cryptographic hashes.

How to do it...

The following are the steps to create a strong hash:

1. Get the password value as plain text.

2. Get a `SHA-1 MessageDigest` instance.

3. Put the `password` string in the `MessageDigest` instance.

4. Execute the `digest` method to get the hash byte array.

5. Encode each byte to a Hexadecimal format into a String Builder.

6. Get the built string from the `StringBuilder` method.

7. The built string is a Hexadecimal representation of the `SHA-1` Hash.

8. The password can now be stored.

In the following screenshot is the code in Java that allows us to create a SHA-1 Hash. It's exactly the same as the MD5 hash, except that we will get a `MessageDigest` instance using the SHA-1 algorithm:

```
public static String getHashSHA1(String password) {
    try {
        MessageDigest md = MessageDigest.getInstance("SHA-1");
        md.update(password.getBytes());
        byte byteData[] = md.digest();
        StringBuilder sb = new StringBuilder();
        for (int i = 0; i < byteData.length; i++) {
            sb.append(Integer.toString(
                    (byteData[i] & 0xff) + 0x100, 16).substring(1));
        }
        return sb.toString();
    } catch (NoSuchAlgorithmException ex) {
        Logger.getLogger("SHA-1").log(Level.SEVERE, null, ex);
        return null;
    }
}
```

Notice that we only changed `MD5` for `SHA-1`, and this produces a stronger hash but the `java.security.MessageDigest` class supports even stronger algorithms. We can use the same code as shown in the preceding screenshot, changing only the algorithm's name for any of the following algorithms (listed from weakest to strongest):

- MD5 (Explained in the first recipe—128 bits Hash)
- SHA-1 (The current recipe—160 bits Hash)
- SHA-256 (Stronger that SHA-1—256 bits Hash)
- SHA-384 (Stronger than SHA-256—384 bits Hash)
- SHA-512 (Stronger than SHA-384—512 bits Hash)

If we create one function for every algorithm, we can compare the resulting hashes and see how different they are:

```
Original Value:
www.packtpub.com
MD5 Hash:
647d0136520b7d08802df7035dccce01
SHA-1 Hash:
e11f183d023e0342cbb3c41b2e5e299a64f76856
SHA-256 Hash:
cd9793342c9c955efd2712bd6c08f1bbf782ab70dc8b31de51ca96c32a4db976
SHA-384 Hash:
60e7a14c1d25b37a579eaad8e9809d07c1be7cc8d0e15b653ff8a856d2e97bad0e55bf5a
656bc9f60d86274eca51d818
SHA-512 Hash:
4962118d0f98152e2e5e829c9889a20fd4ecfd4e5c6981b4cbd1361c03935c6ed4e81e74
cb4efaa5eba0ab7376310609f664e20a466ebcb51789a02f0b22a181
```

In this case, SHA 512 is the stronger plain hash and it's pretty easy to see why.

How it works...

The **Secure Hash Algorithm** (**SHA**) is a family of cryptographic hash algorithms implemented by vendors, designed by the United States **National Security Agency** (**NSA**), and is also used as a standard.

Basically, it works the same way as any other hash function; for variable length data, it generates a unique static length code that we call **hash**. However, these hashes are not always unique; this means that for two different inputs, we could have equal resulting hashes. When this happens, it's called a **collision**.

It's important to note that with a stronger hash, we get lower collision chances. But it's not something to be worried about, at least not too much, because the SHA-256 or higher generates really strong hashes with a very low collision probability, it's highly unlikely to produce a collision.

Still, it's theoretically possible to break a hash and by "breaking a hash," I mean to guess the original word that generates that hash. Actually, it's time to acknowledge that there isn't such a thing as a fully secure hash, because it's always possible to perform a brute-force attack.

A brute-force attack is performed by generating words with the help of a computer, creating a hash for that word, and then comparing it with the stored hash in order to guess the password. However, the idea is to make this kind of attack as expensive, in terms of data processing, as possible. The attacker doesn't want a password 20 years from now; he wants it as soon as possible.

There's more...

The SHA family is far stronger than the MD5 hash function and really expensive to break, at least for now. However, we should never forget what we want to achieve, which is to store our users' passwords in a secure way. But, we are missing something here. We need to ask ourselves, "What kind of passwords do users choose"? Well, the common user chooses easy passwords because they are easier to remember. This is bad for us because an attacker does not even need to perform a brute-force attack; with a simple dictionary-attack he could get hundreds of passwords in minutes!

So remember, even if you decide to use a strong hash function, it's a good idea to require passwords that contain lower and upper case characters as well as numbers and symbols and, of course, a minimum length—long passwords are harder to guess!

Now, if we are storing password hashes generated with a strong algorithm, such as SHA-256 or higher, and a minimum password length combining numbers, symbols, and upper and lower case characters, we can say that our users' passwords are pretty secure. If, somehow, an attacker gains access to those passwords, it will be really hard for him to guess the original password.

However, breaking those passwords is not impossible. Even with good passwords, strong hashes, and all the precautions we have taken, an attacker could still guess the password. It won't be easy for him, but we don't want a "not easy to break". We want to make it almost impossible to break, and in order to do that, we need more than a hashing algorithm and good password: we need to work with our users' data to improve our hash strength—this technique is called **salting**.

Adding salt to a hash (Intermediate)

This recipe teaches how to properly salt hashes to make them even stronger. As you may have guessed, this technique involves adding something to our hashes to make them harder to break.

How to do it...

To sign up or change a password, follow the given steps:

1. Generate a random salt value.
2. Create a MessageDigester with an algorithm you prefer.
3. Add the salt to the MessageDigester .
4. Digest the password with the MessageDigester.
5. Get the hash from the digest.
6. Save the generated salt and the hashed password. In case of sign up, we need to save the username.

To generate a random salt value, consider the code shown in the following screenshot:

```java
public static byte[] getSalt() throws NoSuchAlgorithmException {
    //Always use a secure random generator
    SecureRandom secureRandom = SecureRandom.getInstance("SHA1PRNG");
    //Create array for the salt (16 bytes length)
    byte[] salt = new byte[16];
    //Get a random salt
    secureRandom.nextBytes(salt);
    //Return the generated salt
    return salt;
}
```

We always need to use a `SecureRandom` class to create good salts. In Java, the `SecureRandom` class supports the `"SHA1PRNG"` pseudo random number generator algorithm, and we can take advantage of it. Note that we are returning the salt as a byte array, that's because the `MessageDigest` requires byte arrays. Also, you may have noticed that we created a salt of the size 16 bytes. This is important in order to ensure that our salt is strong enough. Never create a salt shorter than a 16-byte length. This means 128-bit strength (*16 x 8 = 128*) for the salt.

Now that we know how to create the salt, consider the code for creating a hashed password using the salt as shown in the following screenshot:

```
public static byte[] getSaltedHashSHA512(String password, byte[] salt) {
    try {
        //Get a SHA-512 MessageDigest
        MessageDigest md = MessageDigest.getInstance("SHA-512");
        //Add the salt to the MessageDigest
        md.update(salt);
        //Digest the password, notice that we get the password as a byte array
        byte byteData[] = md.digest(password.getBytes());
        //Reset the MessageDigest, just in case
        md.reset();
        //Return the hashed password
        return byteData;
    } catch (NoSuchAlgorithmException ex) {
        Logger.getLogger("SHA-512").log(Level.SEVERE, "SHA-512 is not a valid algorithm name", ex);
        return null;
    }
}
```

Notice that this method receives the `salt` method as a parameter and updates the `MessageDigest` byte buffer with the salt value. After that, it digests the `password` method as a byte array. Internally, it concatenates the salt with the password before digesting.

We can already generate a salt and use it to create a stronger hash, but we will create salts only when the user signs up or when he changes his password. On the other hand, when he authenticates, we need to validate his password. In order to do this, we need to create the same hash, which means that we need to store the salt somewhere.

The following screenshot is just an example of a basic user creation that uses the preceding methods:

```
public static void createUser(String login, String password) {
    // Create a byte array to save the salt
    byte[] byteSalt = null;
    try {
        //Create a new random salt
        byteSalt = getSalt();
    } catch (NoSuchAlgorithmException ex) {
        // This could happen if we choose a not supported algorithm
        Logger.getLogger(SaltUsageSample.class.getName()).log(Level.SEVERE, null, ex);
    }
    //Digest the password with with salt
    byte[] byteDigestPsw = getSaltedHashSHA512(password, byteSalt);
    //Get the hashed password in Base 64
    String strDigestPsw = toHex(byteDigestPsw);
    //Get the salt in base64
    String strSalt = toHex(byteSalt);
    //Create the new user to save the data.
    User user = new User();
    //Now we need to save the following data into a new user:
    //"login" (the login used)
    user.setUsername(login);
    //"strDigestPsw" (hashed password)
    user.setPassword(strDigestPsw);
    //"strSalt" (in order to generate this salted hash again to compare, we will need the original salt
    user.setSalt(strSalt);
    //Save the user into the database
    saveUser(user);
}
```

As you can see, there is a User class. This is just a sample, the User class has a Username, a Password, and a Salt attribute. Also, you may have noticed a new toHex method, which converts a byte array to a hexadecimal string. We will need another fromHex method later, which converts a hexadecimal string to a byte array. The following screenshot is the implementation of these methods:

```java
public static byte[] fromHex(String hex) {
    //Create a byte array with half of the hex string length
    byte[] binary = new byte[hex.length() / 2];
    //For 0 to byte array length
    for (int i = 0; i < binary.length; i++) {
        //Parse 2 chars from base 16 to base 2
        binary[i] = (byte) Integer.parseInt(hex.substring(2 * i, 2 * i + 2), 16);
    }
    //return the byte array
    return binary;
}

public static String toHex(byte[] array) {
    //Create a new BigInteger with the byte array
    BigInteger bi = new BigInteger(1, array);
    //Get the big integer as a string
    String hex = bi.toString(16);
    //Calculate the padding length
    int paddingLength = (array.length * 2) - hex.length();
    //If there is any padding
    if (paddingLength > 0) {
        //Format the padding length and concatenate the hex string
        return String.format("%0" + paddingLength + "d", 0) + hex;
    } else {
        //Else just return the hex string
        return hex;
    }
}
```

The toHex and fromHex methods are implemented in many different libraries and are a standard algorithm. In this example, we have the choice to implement them ourselves to avoid loading any dependencies.

Now that we saw a demonstration of how to create a hash with a salt and saving the generated password and salt we need to check how to validate the user identity when the user logs in.

Consider the following method to validate a user as shown in the screenshot:

```java
public static boolean isValidUser (String login, String password) throws IOException {
    //Retrieve the user from the database
    User user = retrieveUser(login);
    //Get the salt used with the password when the user was created
    String strOriginalSalt = user.getSalt();
    //Get the bytes from the salt, remember it's in hex format
    byte[] byteSalt = fromHex(strOriginalSalt);
    //Digest the login password with the original salt
    byte[] loginPassword = getSaltedHashSHA512(password, byteSalt);
    //Get the stored password for comparing
    byte[] storedPassword = fromHex(user.getPassword());
    //Compare the incoming password with the stored password.
    boolean result = Arrays.equals(loginPassword, storedPassword);
    if (result) {
        System.out.println("Successfull login!");
    } else {
        System.out.println("Login failed!");
    }
    return result;
}
```

As you can see, we retrieve the `user` class from the database and get the original salt to create the hash. After that, we compare the hashes: if they are equal, the password is valid! Note that we use the `fromHex` method here to get the byte array value of hexadecimal strings.

Remember that this is a sample code to show how to use the hash and the salt.

How it works...

When a password is simply hashed, we will eventually realize that identical passwords generate identical hashes—this is not good! Also, plain hashes can be compared with precomputed hashes (also known as rainbow tables).

In order to avoid, or at least make it harder to break our passwords, we can add random data to the original password. This will make every hash different, even if the passwords are the same.

This random data we add is called salt. A salt is a random value of fixed length. The salt generated for a given password must be saved in order to generate the stored hash again.

Now, in the code shown in the preceding screenshot, we are storing the plain salt. This is ok, but it could be better. Consider encrypting the salt with a two-way algorithm in order to have additional protection. Storing it in a different database could also help in making it harder to get. We are not doing that here, but these are very good options to increase security. However, the salt should be pretty secure with a strong hash (SHA-256 or stronger) and a good salt (16 bytes or more). Let's think about this like a hacker: we managed to get the database and the application's source code, but on checking the source code we notice that every single password has a random salt. This means that we can't use rainbow tables. Also, dictionary/brute-force attacks would be really expensive and we would need to get the passwords as soon as possible because someone might notice our intrusion and take measures to prevent such incidents—it's a nightmare!

There's more...

When it comes to salts, there is much misinformation. Salt is a must-do for secure systems, as it is fairly easy to break a weak password even if it's hashed with a secure algorithm. When we add salt to the equation, breaking the password gets significantly harder.

Never re-use a salt, it's pointless. It makes your hashes weak against dictionary, brute-force, and rainbow table attacks. So, salts are not reusable.

Short salts are not an option, salts should be at least 16 bytes length. If we have, let's say, a three character salt, there are only 857.375 (*95 x 95 x 95 = 857.375*) possible salts. Consider that a lookup table with the most common passwords contains around 1024 bytes. This means that the rainbow tables for the possible salts, and the most common passwords would be around 837 GB approximately. Nowadays, that's not a lot.

Crazy hashing and salting

Some people suggest using double hashing techniques or mixing different hashing algorithms and then creating a new hash with the digests. Although this may work, it's not a good option and I do not recommend it. There are other standards and well-tested techniques to make our hashes even stronger, so avoid trying to create your own technique.

Creating a secure hash (Advanced)

This recipe teaches us how to create a truly secure strong hash and how to strengthen it as computers becomes more capable of breaking it.

There are libraries that provide secure hash functionality, but we are going to use a standard, plain java algorithm named `PBKDF2WithHmacSHA1`. So, we won't need any third-party libraries.

How to do it...

To create the first hash (Sign up), follow the given steps:

1. Get the password as a char array.

2. Create a salt value.

3. Create a password based encryption key spec.

4. Create a key factory.

5. Generate the hash.

6. Add the iterations and the original salt to your hash.

To generate a strong hash, please consider the code shown in the following screenshot:

```
public static String generateStrongHash(String password) throws NoSuchAlgorithmException, InvalidKeySpecException {
    // We want iterate over the hash lots of times, to make it harder to crack...
    int iterations = 1000;
    //... Get the password as a char array
    char[] passwordAsCharArray = password.toCharArray();
    //... Create a byte array to save the salt
    byte[] salt = getSalt();
    //... Create a password-based encryption key spec
    // It needs the password to hash as a char array, the salt as a byte array, the amount of iterations,
    // and the amount of bits (64 bytes * 8 bits = 512 bits itam)
    PBEKeySpec spec = new PBEKeySpec(passwordAsCharArray, salt, iterations, 64 * 8);
    //... Create a secret key factory for the "PBKDF2WithHmacSHA1" algorithm
    SecretKeyFactory skf = SecretKeyFactory.getInstance("PBKDF2WithHmacSHA1");
    //... Compute the password to generate a hash
    byte[] hash = skf.generateSecret(spec).getEncoded();
    //... Return the generated hash, formatted as 'iterations:salt:hash'
    return iterations + ":" + toHex(salt) + ":" + toHex(hash);
}
```

We can test it by running the code shown in the following screenshot:

```
public static void main(String[] args) throws NoSuchAlgorithmException, InvalidKeySpecException {
    String password = "www.packtpub.com";
    System.out.println("Password: " + password);
    System.out.println("Hash (formatted 'iterations:salt:hash'" + generateStrongHash(password));
}
```

It should print the result as shown in the following screenshot:

```
Password: www.packtpub.com
Hash (formatted 'iterations:salt:hash'):  1000:ffd0236a2fe202f2374786bce5aab61fe99b9208015b8
899:d23a8dc3834d53cbf213cc0f329fe61e3188954809b6c57d6177890f52db56d0c71dealb73bba52940f82a93
676b9572069e8497459d3f48277eeb85abc0f6ac
```

For the `getSalt` function, consider the code shown in the following screenshot:

```java
public static byte[] getSalt() throws NoSuchAlgorithmException {
    //Always use a secure random generator
    SecureRandom secureRandom = SecureRandom.getInstance("SHA1PRNG");
    //Create array for the salt (16 bytes length)
    byte[] salt = new byte[16];
    //Get a random salt
    secureRandom.nextBytes(salt);
    //Return the generated salt
    return salt;
}
```

Also, consider the following code for the `toHex` and `fromHex` functions:

```java
public static byte[] fromHex(String hex) {
    //Create a byte array with half of the hex string length
    byte[] binary = new byte[hex.length() / 2];
    //For 0 to byte array length
    for (int i = 0; i < binary.length; i++) {
        //Parse 2 chars from base 16 to base 2
        binary[i] = (byte) Integer.parseInt(hex.substring(2 * i, 2 * i + 2), 16);
    }
    //return the byte array
    return binary;
}

public static String toHex(byte[] array) {
    //Create a new BigInteger with the byte array
    BigInteger bi = new BigInteger(1, array);
    //Get the big integer as a string
    String hex = bi.toString(16);
    //Calculate the padding length
    int paddingLength = (array.length * 2) - hex.length();
    //If there is any padding
    if (paddingLength > 0) {
        //Format the padding length and concatenate the hex string
        return String.format("%0" + paddingLength + "d", 0) + hex;
    } else {
        //Else just return the hex string
        return hex;
    }
}
```

This was pretty easy considering it's generating a really strong hash! Keep in mind that this code is just an example, for real development it should be coded in a maintainable way.

Now, we've just seen how to create the password hash. This is useful for creating a new user with a new password, or changing the old password for a new one, but how about authentication?

To compare hashes (Authentication), follow the given steps:

1. Get the password as a char array.

2. Get the stored password with its iterations and salt.

3. Create a password-based encryption key spec.

4. Create a key factory.

5. Generate the hash formatted with the salt and the iterations.

6. Compare the generated hash with the stored one.

Consider the code shown in the following screenshot, which is used to validate a user:

```
public static Boolean isValidUser(String password, String storedAuthentication) throws NoSuchAlgorithmException, InvalidKeySpecException {

    char[] passwordAsCharArray = password.toCharArray();

    String[] params = storedAuthentication.split(":");

    int iterations = Integer.parseInt(params[0]);

    byte[] salt = fromHex(params[1]);

    byte[] hash = fromHex(params[2]);

    PBEKeySpec spec = new PBEKeySpec(passwordAsCharArray, salt, iterations, hash.length);

    SecretKeyFactory skf = SecretKeyFactory.getInstance("PBKDF2WithHmacSHA1");

    byte[] testHash = skf.generateSecret(spec).getEncoded();

    return slowEquals(hash, testHash);
}
```

As you can see, it returns a Boolean value: `true` when the password is valid, `false` when the password is invalid.

You probably noticed a new function here named `slowEquals`. This function performs a length-constant time comparison in order to avoid timing attacks. It is a theoretical attack and I seriously doubt whether it could be done over the internet, but it's nice to be aware of the `slowEquals` function.

Consider the following code that performs a length-constant time comparison:

```
private static boolean slowEquals(byte[] a, byte[] b) {
    //Store the variable diff the diference between the length of the byte array "a"
    //and the length of the byte array "b"
    //if they are equal this will get a zero value
    int diff = a.length ^ b.length;
    // Iterates over both arrays and compares each byte
    for (int i = 0; i < a.length && i < b.length; i++) {
        // Inclusive assignment(if diff == 0, it assigns to diff the result of comparing two bytes,
        // if they are equal it assigns a 0, else another number)
        diff |= a[i] ^ b[i];
    }
    //Returns the result of comparing diff to 0 (if there are no differences it will return true)
    return diff == 0;
}
```

That's it! We can now generate and validate passwords in a secure way; and even better, as technology evolves, we can increase the amount of iterations in order to make our hashes stronger!

How it works...

We've seen that salting help us to make it harder to break our hashes, and it's impractical to use rainbow tables or dictionaries. However, salting does not protect against brute-force attacks since SHA algorithms are designed to be fast; as technology evolves, these hashes will be broken eventually. To make these attacks less effective, we can use a technique known as key stretching.

The idea is to make the hash function more long and complex. So, even with a fast CPU or custom hardware, dictionary and brute-force attacks are too slow to be worthwhile. The goal is to make the hash function slow enough to impede attacks, but still fast enough to not cause a noticeable delay for the user.

Key stretching is implemented using a special type of CPU-intensive hash function. Don't try to invent your own. Simply hashing the hash of the password iteratively isn't enough as it can be parallelized in hardware and executed as fast as a normal hash. Use a standard algorithm like PBKDF2 (the one we used), Bcrypt, or Scrypt. These are very strong and well-tested algorithms.

These algorithms take a work factor (also known as security factor) or iteration count as an argument. This value determines how slow the hash function will be. When computers become faster next year, we can increase the work factor.

There's more...

It's important to remember that hashing is the last defense, and as such we should use the best protection available because if an intrusion happens, we will need it.

Also, if an intrusion does happen, there are several things we must do as responsible IT professionals:

- Determine how the system was compromised and patch the vulnerability as soon as possible.

- Inform your users right away: even if we don't fully understand how it happened, our users need to know about it.

- Explain how the passwords were protected and encourage your users to change similar passwords in different websites, because malicious hackers usually try any password they can find in different sites.

- It's possible, even with salted hashes, that an attacker will be able to crack some weak passwords. To reduce the attacker's window, it would be good to implement an e-mail loop authentication.

- Also, our users need to know what personal information was stored on the website. For example, we should instruct users to look over recent and future bills if we have credit card details stored.

Overview

This chapter involves a high level overview to round up the complete authentication process.

Rounding up...

We have now successfully learned how to secure our users' passwords using hashes; however, we should take a look at the big picture, just in case. The following figure shows what a very basic web application looks like:

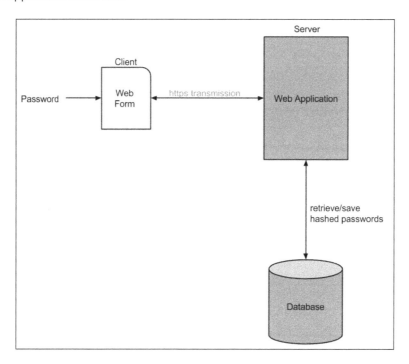

Note the **https transmission** tag: HTTPS is a secure transfer protocol, which allows us to transport information in a secure way. When we transport sensitive data such as passwords in a **Web Application**, anyone who intercepts the connection can easily get the password in plain text, and our users' data would be compromised. We will cover SSL, HTTPS, and TLS in detail at the end of this chapter.

In order to avoid this, we should always use HTTPS when there's sensitive data involved. HTTPS is fairly easy to setup, you just need to buy an SSL certificate and configure it with your hosting provider. Configuration varies depending on the provider, but usually they provide an easy way to do it.

It is strongly suggested to use HTTPS for authentication, sign up, sign in, and other sensitive data processes. As a general rule, most (if not all) of the data exchange that requires the user to be logged in should be protected. Keep in mind that HTTPS comes at a cost, so try to avoid using HTTPS on static pages that have public information.

Always keep in mind that to protect the password, we need ensure secure transport (with HTTPS) and secure storage (with strong hashes) as well. Both are critical phases and we need to be very careful with them.

Now that our passwords and other sensitive data are being transferred in a secure way, we can get into the application workflow. Consider the following steps for an authentication process:

1. The application receives an **Authentication Request**.

2. The **Web Layer** takes care of it as it gets the parameters (username and password), and passes them to the **Authentication Service**.

3. The Authentication Service calls the **Database Access Layer** to retrieve the user from the database.

4. The Database Access Layer queries the database, gets the user, and returns it to the Authentication Service.

5. The Authentication Service gets the stored hash from the users' data retrieved from the database, extracts the salt and the amount of iterations, and calls the **Hashing Utility** passing the password from the authentication request, the salt, and the iterations.

6. The Hashing Utility generates the hash and returns it to the Authentication Service.

7. The Authentication Service performs a constant-time comparison between the stored hash and the generated hash, and we inform the Web Layer if the user is authenticated or not.

8. The Web Layer returns the corresponding view to the user depending on whether they are authenticated or not.

The following figure can help us understand how this works, please consider that flows **1**, **2**, **3**, and **4** are bidirectional:

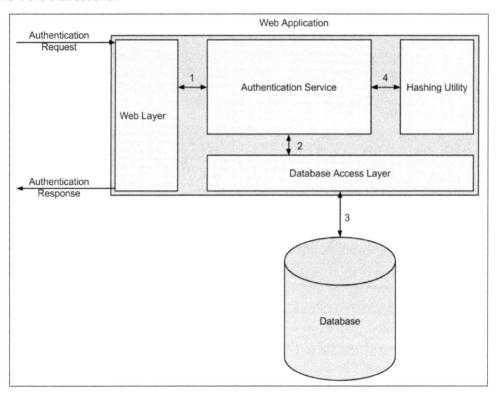

The Authentication Service and the Hashing Utility components are the ones we have been working with so far. We already know how to create hashes, this workflow is an example to understand when we should it.

More Info: Hyper Text Transfer Protocol Secure (HTTPS)

The HTTPS is a communication protocol that is used for secure communication. Technically, it is the result of layering the HTTP on top of the SSL/TLS protocol. It uses symmetric keys to encrypt the data flow between client and server. The symmetric keys are exchanged using X.509 certificates and hence asymmetric cryptography is used during the initial communication. It requires an SSL certificate, which contains the necessary public key and the identity of the owner. The matching private key is not available publicly. Anyone can generate an SSL certificate; however, with self-generated certificates, the relation between the owner of the certificate and the certificate itself can't be verified. Self-generated certificates are used for development/testing purposes. In order to validate the relation between the owner of the certificate and the certificate, there are certificate authorities who provide reliable digital certificates.

A Certificate Authority (also known as CA) is an entity that provides digital certificates. The CA is trusted by the owner of the certificate and those relying upon the certificate. There are commercial CAs that sell certificates, and some providers issue them for free. Large institutions and government entities may have their own CAs. Getting a certificate involves creating a **Certificate Signing Request** (**CSR**) for your server. You need a CA to sign it; the CA will need to validate that you are indeed the owner of the domain. To authenticate the owner of the certificate, most CAs perform a Domain Validation. It involves sending an e-mail to validate the recipient, or logging in with your domain name provider. The process varies according to the CA and the level of security of the certificate. Higher levels of security involve a more extensive validation process.

When the process is finished, the certificate is a digital proof that the web domain is authentic, and that it has been validated by a trusted third party. There are three versions of the SSL protocol. The Version 1.0 was never released to the public; on the other hand, Version 2.0 was released to the public but it had some critical flaws and was replaced by Version 3.0 shortly after.

Transport Layer Security (**TLS**) had three versions at that time; Version 1.0 is an upgrade to SSL 3.0 and includes TLS/SSL interoperability. This means that a TLS implementation can be downgraded to SSL 3.0 if the browser does not support TLS. TLS 1.1 is an update, which includes, among other minor improvements, a protection against **Cipher Block Chaining** (**CBC**) attacks and supports **Internet Assigned Numbers Authority** (**IANA**) registration parameters. TLS 1.2 includes some major improvements over the TLS 1.1, including stronger hashes that improve security, enhancements in server-client communication, and better support for different ciphers.

Basically, this is how SSL/TLS works:

- A **Client** sends a "Hello!" message along with the necessary information and data to begin the secure communication.
- The **Server** responds with a "Hello!" message, specifying the chosen protocol, some other necessary information, and the certificate (the last one depends on the cipher suite).
- The Client responds with a **Key Exchange** message. It may contain a master secret key, a public key, or nothing (again, this depends on the cipher suite). If there's no master secret key, then the Client and the Server generate a common secret key.
- The Client sends a record to the Server, informing him that everything it sends from now on will be encrypted.
- The Server confirms that everything he sends from now on will also be encrypted.
- Now the Client and Server can exchange data in a secure way.

The following figure illustrates this interaction:

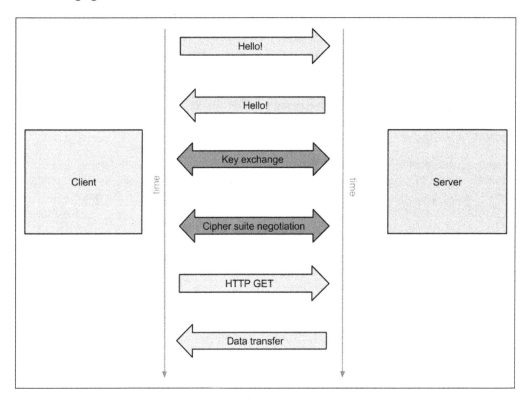

Thus, we have gone through the process of authentication.

Thank you for buying
Instant Java Password and Authentication Security

About Packt Publishing

Packt, pronounced 'packed', published its first book "*Mastering phpMyAdmin for Effective MySQL Management*" in April 2004 and subsequently continued to specialize in publishing highly focused books on specific technologies and solutions.

Our books and publications share the experiences of your fellow IT professionals in adapting and customizing today's systems, applications, and frameworks. Our solution based books give you the knowledge and power to customize the software and technologies you're using to get the job done. Packt books are more specific and less general than the IT books you have seen in the past. Our unique business model allows us to bring you more focused information, giving you more of what you need to know, and less of what you don't.

Packt is a modern, yet unique publishing company, which focuses on producing quality, cutting-edge books for communities of developers, administrators, and newbies alike. For more information, please visit our website: www.packtpub.com.

Writing for Packt

We welcome all inquiries from people who are interested in authoring. Book proposals should be sent to author@packtpub.com. If your book idea is still at an early stage and you would like to discuss it first before writing a formal book proposal, contact us; one of our commissioning editors will get in touch with you.

We're not just looking for published authors; if you have strong technical skills but no writing experience, our experienced editors can help you develop a writing career, or simply get some additional reward for your expertise.

ModSecurity 2.5

ISBN: 978-1-84719-474-9   Paperback: 280 pages

Prevent web application hacking with this easy to use guide

1. Secure your system by knowing exactly how a hacker would break into it

2. Covers writing rules in-depth and Modsecurity rule language elements such as variables, actions, and request phases

3. Covers the common attacks in use on the Web, and ways to find the geographical location of an attacker and send alert emails when attacks are discovered

Mobile Security: How to Secure, Privatize, and Recover Your Devices

ISBN: 9781-8-4969-360-8   Paperback: 242 pages

Keep your data secure on the go

1. Learn how mobile devices are monitored and the impact of cloud computing

2. Understand the attacks hackers use and how to prevent them

3. Keep yourself and your loved ones safe online

Please check **www.PacktPub.com** for information on our titles

www.ingramcontent.com/pod-product-compliance
Lightning Source LLC
LaVergne TN
LVHW080106070326
832902LV00014B/2457

* 9 7 8 1 8 4 9 6 9 7 7 6 7 *